# Cold Cash
## by Christopher Lc

# Cold Ca$h

## Christopher Lamparello

Revised edition

## City Books Publishing Company

18 Greenwich Avenue, Suite 185
New York, NY 10011

This publication is designed to provide accurate and authoritative information in regard to the subject matter covered. It is sold with the understanding that the publisher and author are not engaged in rendering legal, accounting or other professional service. If legal advice or other expert assistance is required, the services of a competent professional person should be sought.

FROM A DECLARATION OF PRINCIPLES JOINTLY ADOPTED BY A COMMITTEE OF THE AMERICAN BAR ASSOCIATION AND A COMMITTEE OF PUBLISHERS.

Printed in the United States of America; First printing, June, 1995. First printing of revised edition, June, 1996

# Introduction

The book that you are holding has the power to change your entire financial future. I know this because the ideas discussed within these pages have had a profound effect on my own life. They opened my eyes to an exciting arena of wealth that I never before knew existed. They have also provided a lot of excitement, enjoyment and fun. I can say without fear of contradiction that the system contained in this book is actually a hobby for me. That's how enjoyable it is. My journey on the road to wealth has not always been easy, however.

I remember when I was a young fourteen-year old boy. I was already excited about money making opportunities. I guess I had acquired the "entrepreneurial spirit" early on in life, so I regularly purchased issues of popular money making magazines. Inside one such magazine was a full page ad promising that within 90 days, I would earn over $100,000 with no effort on my part *or* any investment. At fourteen years old, I was extremely excited and immediately ran to the post office and sent out a money order, eagerly awaiting the arrival of my new life.

You may be able to predict the rest of my adventure! About four weeks later, a pamphlet arrived in the mail. It was about twenty pages long, if that. The system that was supposed to make me so rich turned out to be a scheme on holding garage sales! The author said that anyone could hold a garage sale and make a fortune every weekend. The idea seemed so ridiculous to me that I had a tough time understanding how anyone could market such a system with good conscience. Obviously, I was very disappointed. About thirty minutes later, when I finished reading the pamphlet, I began to realize that making money is, in reality, a very daunting task. It requires dedication and a willingness to persist that, unfortunately, most human beings simply do not possess within themselves.

Remembering the lesson I learned as a child, I know that the reason you purchased this manual was not to receive pictures and a lot of silliness, but to get real advice on building a lucrative, serious business that has a proven track record for creating wealth. I believe that what you will find within the pages of this manual will enlighten, excite and maybe even captivate you. Indeed, this publication is filled with very powerful information that can change your financial future. I have provided the facts. You need to provide the necessary enthusiasm.

You may be undergoing difficult times financially. Or, perhaps you are in need of an extra or second income. Whatever your needs, this system can provide you with the earnings that you desire. If you wish to use it full-time, you can make a real, full-time income. As with any business, this may not happen immediately at first. As you become more comfortable with its use, however, you'll begin to master it, and you may decide to make it your life's work. I know many people who have done just that and are loving it!

On the other hand, you may apply the system part time and receive a handsome second income in return. Many individuals, in fact, begin by using the system as a sideline business and soon discover, much to their pleasure, that it can provide an excellent full-time income. You may decide to begin this way. This is perfectly legitimate and even advisable. If things go well for you, as I expect they will, you can always quit your job and apply the system full-time later.

This is not a "pie-in-the-sky" idea. It's a real business that people are profiting from everyday. I have personally witnessed individuals make a five minute phone call at ten o'clock in the morning and receive two-thousand dollars in profits by the time lunch is ready. This is not an exaggeration. It is being done every single day and it will continue to be accomplished on a daily basis in this business. It is completely normal to hear stories of these kinds of amazing profits. You can do this too.

You will find the Cold Cash system to be very different from any other way of making money that you have researched in the past. It is a serious business for dedicated individuals. If you have a goal of financial freedom and you are willing to devote the necessary time and energy to make it successful, you may soon find that your life has changed forever. Many have said that the system contained within these pages is one of the finest strategies for obtaining wealth in the world. I believe this to be true. I do know that I have seen this system work as no other one could. Best of all, it has worked for all types of people, from all walks of life. No matter who you may be, it can work for you.

This is good news in a field where a disturbing trend has developed within the last few years. Many of the so-called wealth opportunities that are published today are absolutely unworkable, untested and unreliable. Some are so bad, in fact, that those who participate in them are probably doomed to lose their entire investment, simply because they thought that they were receiving reliable information when, in reality, they were not. This book is entirely different from the rest of the plans that are currently available in the opportunity field. Read this manual for yourself and put the system to use. I believe that you'll be extremely pleased with the results.

The *Cold Cash* manual has been divided into two sections. Book one describes a system that you can use to make hundreds of dollars (or even thousands) from one five-minute phone call! With a very tiny investment, you may well be on your way to *Cold Cash* riches! Book two offers another five-minute phone call system that differs from the first. If you're the type of person who likes a challenge, the bonus system will offer some insightful knowledge into how you can use your abilities to line your pocketbook with cash.

I know why you're reading this book. I only ask you one favor. Don't skim through the book and put it away. If you do that, you'll never reach your dream of financial success. Also, don't read it through and decide it's not for you and return it. Trust me, this book may well be worth its weight in gold to you someday. The systems described are extremely valuable, and you never know when a day will come along when you have a chance to use them. Let me give you an example.

A woman, who I'll refer to as Sharon, called me the other day and related an amazing story. Some time ago, she had seen the advertisement for this book and had ordered it immediately. After sending in her payment, Sharon received the *Cold Cash* manual shortly thereafter. She read it through and thought that it had some good ideas, but, for some reason, it just wasn't for her.

She didn't have any money at all, so she decided to return the manual.

Two weeks later, Sharon was in Atlantic City. You may know that Atlantic City is filled with casinos, and, after receiving her paycheck, she decided to take fifty dollars and play the slot machines. As a businessman, I must tell you that I don't think gambling is a good idea. Most people walk away losers, as the entire casino is, for the most part, heavily slanted towards the house. Anyway, to continue my story, Sharon won $300 on the slot machines. She ran home with the money, knowing that she would use it for her new business.

She thought of the *Cold Cash* system and decided that she would use it immediately. When she got home, however, she remembered that she had sent it back. Frustrated, she called our company and reordered it. Sharon told me that waiting ten days for her second copy to arrive was sheer torture! When she did receive it, however, she carefully followed the instructions and turned her slot machine winnings into real profit.

My point should be obvious. **This is a proven system.** It may not be what you think you'll be doing, but, as Sharon's story shows us, when information is good and worthwhile, it's right and proper to hang onto it. Your circumstances can change. Your opinions can change. You might meet someone who knows just the thing to do. Therefore, keep building your arsenal of money information and understand that **this book** can totally change your future. It can do it today, it can do it next month, or it can do it in a year. But it can do it!

# Chapter One
## The Recipe for Riches

Some time ago, I heard a man say that you need money to make money. To some extent, this is true. Every opportunity usually requires at least a small amount of money to get off the ground. There are, however, other things that are more important than money if you hope to reach your goal of wealth.

"More important than money?" you ask. Yes, there are ingredients to success that are more important than money. Without these ingredients, you could start off with millions of dollars and eventually wind up broke. With these ingredients, however, you can start off with virtually no money and wind up richer than you've ever imagined.

These three magical ingredients are *desire, action* and *perseverance.* If you do not have these elements, your quest for wealth will be lost. They are essential to any American Dream. They are so powerful that nothing can stop a man or woman who is determined to use them to their full potential. Put together, they are more powerful than dynamite.

Firstly, desire. Desire can be one of the most haunting emotions. It reminds you of the things that you do not have, for if you had them, you would not desire them. Desire that is not channeled into any positive activity will soon weaken, but desire that is turned into action will free a man or woman from the chains of poverty and despair. If you are an individual with a strong *desire* to grow rich, you have completed the first step towards wealth. You must now turn your desire into the next step, *action*. If you so strongly desire something, it only makes logical sense to take action towards obtaining what you desire. It takes a great deal of action to acquire money, so it is essential that you continually make new efforts towards attaining your goal. Someday, one of your efforts will pay off.

No matter what business you are in, you will not succeed without action. Nothing in life changes without action. Action leads to great and wonderful things, while inaction leads to unhappiness and defeat. If you are upset about your circumstances, change your despair into *desire and action*. Doing this will change your entire life. Everyone runs into bad circumstances, but those who persevere are the ones who come through with flying colors.

Perseverance is the third and final ingredient for success. This means "not giving up." If you have desire and action in your life, perseverance is the last and final ingredient that you must obtain before you reach your goal of monetary wealth. When you translate your desire into action, there will be times that you will not be successful. A new business fails, or an interesting idea falls through. It has happened to virtually every man and woman on the earth. It is during these times that perseverance will carry you through the storm and plant your feet on dry ground. It is at this point that the successful individual will pick right up and begin another action while the unsuccessful one will become discouraged and will stop taking action to obtain his or her dream.

You have a dream. That is the reason you purchased this book. Your dream is that you want your financial situation to change. You want things to get better. The good news is that your financial situation *will* change if you are willing to make the three ingredients of success a rule in your life. Concentrate on your goal and work up the desire to change your life. Then, translate the desire into action. Should that action fail, use ingredient three and *persevere*. If you are willing to persevere, you can obtain your desire.

Do you ever wonder why some people prosper while you do not? The reason is simple. Successful people are determined to become wealthy, and they don't stop trying until they have succeeded. If they should fail at a project, they examine their mistakes and educate themselves. When it comes time to pick themselves up after a defeat, successful people don't even think twice. They immediately begin working on a new project that they hope will fulfill their dreams. Prosperous people do not have to be convinced to take action. After a failure, they do it almost automatically.

Some of the wealthiest individuals in the world were born the poorest in the world. This is proof that the three ingredients to success are the most powerful elements in the world. They can move mountains. They are an invaluable tool as you travel down the road to wealth. Use them and you will prosper financially like you never thought before. If you want to keep your dream of financial freedom alive, use the recipe for riches. If you follow it, it will not fail you.

In addition to the Recipe for Riches, you should also be in a good psychological frame of mind before you can receive wealth. I have seen people with great talents who were psychologically unable to receive wealth because they thought that they were undeserving in some sense or another. Conversely, I have known people of average intelligence who have made quick fortunes, apparently with moderate or even very little outward effort!

The reason for this is simple. Let me ask you a question. What do you believe about money? The question may sound unusual at first, but believe me, it's one of the most important questions that you can ask yourself. You see, society has done quite well in convincing people that money is a bad thing. Governments demand that the "rich" get taxed at a higher rate. Religions declare that money is evil, and individuals allow themselves to believe that they are not personally deserving of wealth.

As difficult as it may be, and as much effort as it may require, it is imperative that you discard your negative ideas about money. I have never seen a successful person who felt "unworthy" to receive big money. The two factors go hand-in-hand. You cannot become rich while, at the same time, you still believe that money is wrong or evil. If you believe, as so many people do, that rich people are miserable and that the "poor" are the only happy people around, you're denying yourself an opportunity to change your entire financial future.

No system will work as long as you hold onto these kinds of beliefs. You have to understand that every single human being is entitled to a comfortable lifestyle. The only good that can come from money is that it can open you up to an entire new array of experiences. It's the experience of having money that you desire, not the money itself. Money is merely green ink on government paper. It is what money can do for you that should make you enthusiastic about attaining wealth.

You'll be able to supply for yourself like never before. You'll replace the bad experience of running out of money before your next paycheck with the new and stimulating experience of having more money than you could possibly spend. But in order to achieve this status, you must abandon your negative ideas about money. Money is not evil. People who make money are not evil. Having money does not make you "responsible" for the hungry masses in the world. Money is just green paper that can provide you with new experiences. Open your mind up to the idea that you, no matter who you are, are entitled to receive money and to live a comfortable life. Whatever you may have been taught about money is probably wrong. Money is there for your enjoyment, and you should have no difficulty in believing that you deserve to receive it plentifully.

If your mind believes that you do not "deserve" to receive big money, you never will. You must first believe that you, as a human being, are entitled to wealth before you actually begin to receive it. You should dispel all of the negative emotions that may come your way, such as guilt, embarrassment, and shame. There is nothing "good" about being poor. Being poor is a pitiful thing that no person should have to experience.

Many people fail in their efforts to become independently wealthy because they fail to begin this important first step before they attempt to make money. Before you invest any money in any project, free your mind from the chains that society has placed there. Once you truly begin to believe that you are entitled to wealth, it will follow.  Dozens of new millionaires are made everyday in the United States of America.  Why not be the next one?

# Chapter Two
## Beginning your business

I know you've been wondering how it could ever be possible to make hundreds of dollars from one simple five-minute phone call. As you will soon see, it's easier than you think. Before getting into the system, however, read the introduction that precedes this chapter, if you have yet to. It contains valuable information that can have an impact on your business success, so please don't forsake it.

I know that you purchased this book because you need to change your financial situation. Believe me, I think about you and people like you all the time. Through my phone conversations with people from all over the world, I've come to know what type of situation you're in, and what it will take to get you out of it. I have been where you are, and I know what works and what doesn't work.

I personally purchase dozens of work at home systems, just to see what's currently selling on the market. I will often receive something in the mail that startles or even shocks me. I've even received systems that were downright illegal. I've even received the same book **four times... all from different advertisements!** Probably the worst systems I receive aren't the illegal ones or the same ones. The ones that irk me the most are the difficult and confusing ones. I know that you're looking for something that works. It has to meet the specifications of your situation. It should be...

- **Easy to do;**
- **Inexpensive to begin, while realizing that any true business opportunity requires some sort of investment;**
- **Easy to understand;**
- **Profitable right from the beginning;**
- **If possible, enjoyable;**

The business that we're about to discuss meets all of the criteria above. Not only is it easy to do and enjoyable, but you can begin with a small investment and start making money right away. You may not make thousands of dollars on your first five-minute phone call, but you can easily work your way up to that within a few weeks if you dedicate your time and energy towards your goal of wealth.

When starting any business, **effort and dedication** are needed. If you aren't willing to give **any** business plan your "all," you'll never achieve financial freedom. I hope that doesn't sound harsh, because it's the truth. While the *Cold Cash* system is one of the easiest business plans that I've ever seen, I can tell you that even this plan requires a certain degree of effort and willingness to overcome any initial failures that you may experience in the beginning.

This business can change your entire life. I know people who are involved in this business who love making hundreds, even thousands of dollars from their five-minute phone call business. Trust me, it's a great feeling to hang up the phone and know that a check is on its way to your mailbox. The business that can help you achieve your goals is called contracting.

## What IS contracting?

Contracting is quite simple, and anyone can do it. It simply involves bringing two people together (a buyer and a seller) and collecting a fee when the buyer and seller strike a deal. The *Cold Cash* plan is unique because it utilizes a proven business but changes it just a bit so that anyone, regardless of education or income, can begin immediately without having to leave their homes. Therefore, I'm going to ask you to forget everything you've ever been told about contracting and begin with a fresh, open mind.

In today's fast-paced world, there are many people who need services. There are people who need plumbers, carpenters, electricians, locksmiths, and many other types of important services, oftentimes in an emergency. What happens if the pipes under your sink spring a leak? You call your plumber, of course. Many people, however, don't have a regular plumber to call. They often run to their local yellow pages and call the first number they see.

Remember, contracting isn't limited to plumbing. I'm just using it as an example. There are a variety of services that can be contracted out. This is where you come in. I'm going to show how you can do this in your spare time and even build it up to a full-time income. I've known people who quit their jobs **after their first five minute phone call!**

It's not a fantasy. I've seen it happen more than once in this business. You can literally make hundreds of dollars from one five-minute phone call. As with any business, however, it's important to do things right. I'm going to show you how to begin your new business in such a way as to maximize your chances for success. Since I don't know you, I can't take personal responsibility for your results, but I can show you what I've learned about this business and encourage you to try to do as well as you can do, and that may well result in your achieving all of the goals you've found so elusive thus far.

Before you begin receiving your five-minute phone calls, you have to select a service that you're going to offer. **You will never actually perform any service for your customers other than connecting them with someone who can give them what they need.** This is important. You will never have to get your hands dirty doing any kind of work that you aren't trained to do. You'll leave that to the professionals. You have a choice of what services you can offer. It really depends upon what the needs of your community are and what services are most popular.

Allow me to continue using plumbing as an example. I live in New York City, and there are a lot of plumbers here. More importantly, there's a real need for plumbing. People have plumbing emergencies all the time, and they need someone fast. This is where your service comes in. People will see your plumbing ad and will call you. You'll connect them up with a plumber and receive a nice commission check from the plumbing service for your trouble! Of course, there are a few things you have to take care of first before you're in a position to begin receiving phone calls. I promised you that I would explain everything I know about this business, and I'm not about to expect you to figure it all out on your own. Right now, you'll need to complete the following steps. Don't do any of these steps now. We'll discuss them in greater detail later.

- **Select a service;**
- **Contact service providers who agree to a commission deal;**
- **Write your ad;**
- **Place your ad in local newspapers;**
- **Begin receiving phone calls!**

The above steps are quite simple, but you will need to devote some time to taking care of them before you can begin receiving your special five-minute phone calls.

## Selecting a service

The service that you're going to offer should be something that people in your community need. You can choose plumbing, locksmith service, taxi service, electrician service, appliance repair or any **service** that people in your community can use. You'll be placing ads that offer your service, so make sure it's something that is both in demand and something you're comfortable with. If you have some knowledge of any of these services, that's all the better, but it's not necessary. The service you choose should be somewhat costly, so you'll receive decent commissions. It should also be widely used so demand does exist. You'll be sending the service supplier your caller's business and, soon thereafter, you'll receive a commission check for your share of the fee.

## Contacting service providers

After you decide upon a service that you'll be contracting out, contact as many providers in your area as you can and tell them about your new business. A typical phone conversation may go something like the following:

**You:**    Hello, may I speak to the owner of *Pete's Plumbing Service?* My name is John

**26**

|         |                                                                 |
|---------|-----------------------------------------------------------------|
|         | Smith and I have something important to mention to him.         |
| **Owner:** | Hello, this is Pete. Who are you?                            |
| **You:** | Pete, my name is John Smith and I have a small contracting firm here in Mapleville. We have people in our area who need plumbing service, and they call us and ask for a plumber. |
| **Owner:** | So what does this have to do with me?                       |
| **You:** | I'd like to know if you'd like to take some of the plumbing jobs that come my way. The people I have right now can't handle the work themselves, so I've chosen your fine company to take it on. |
| **Owner:** | What's in it for me?                                        |
| **You:** | Of course, you can continue to charge your rates as you usually charge. |
| **Owner:** | Yeah, right, but what's in it for **you?**                  |
| **You:** | Of course, since we'll be taking all of the phone calls and arranging all of the jobs with the customer, we ask a 20% commission on each job. We think that's fair. So, would you like to get started? I'm sure this will bring in a lot of business for your plumbing company. |

See how it works? It's not difficult at all. You simply have to choose a service, and, once you've signed up as many providers of that service as you can, you're ready to begin taking orders (and big commissions!). It's best to contact as many service providers as possible **in the areas that you'll be placing your ads.** If your local newspaper covers five towns, get out the yellow pages and call as many service providers from those five areas and try to sign them up. All you need is one service provider and you're in business.

It shouldn't prove overly difficult to get a few service providers on your commission list. After all, you'll be sending them a lot of business. Nonetheless, however, you will encounter some services that don't want your help in getting customers. Don't let this discourage you, however. We live in a world where many different types of people exist, and some may simply not feel comfortable entering into an agreement with an outside company. Some others may yet tell you "no" for literally no reason at all! This is how things work in the business world, and you shouldn't think that you're the reason for every negative response. The most important thing to do will be to keep calling various service providers. Make a list of all of the various service providers in the areas you'll be advertising in and begin calling your list.

## Making your commission list

When you call the various companies on your list, record their answers carefully. You may get a definite "no" from some, a definite "yes" from others, and an answer somewhere in between from still others. Record these answers carefully. You'll need to refer back to your list to see what companies you should keep calling, what companies you should give up on, and what companies you can add to your commission list. Your commission list will be a list of all of the companies that have said "yes" to your offer of sending customers their way. You'll be earning commissions from these companies, so careful record-keeping is essential.

Keep calling as many companies as you can find in your area and even in the surrounding areas in the event that someone from those parts should see your ad and call for service. Remember, it doesn't cost you anything if you sign up too **many** services. If you do sign up too many, you'll simply not do much business with the ones that aren't needed. No loss for you. If, however, you sign up too few companies, you'll have to turn business away if things get busy, and that will cost you profits. **After** your commission list is compiled, it should look something like this:

**Mike's Plumbing**
**(212) 555-8783**

**John's Plumbing and Repair Service**
**(212) 555-2946**

**King Plumbing**
**(212) 555-1373**

**Quick Plumbing Company**
**(212) 555-9893**

Your list may be larger than the sample I've provided here, but for sake of discussion, notice that I've listed the exact name of each plumber as well as their phone number. You should keep their addresses separately. After your list is completed, you're ready to begin receiving phone calls and commission checks. Before you do, however, there are a couple of things that should be taken care of first.

### Asking for a price list

When you sign a company onto your commission list, ask them to send you a price list of their services, so you'll know what prices to quote on certain jobs. Often, companies will tell you that there is no price list, that specific prices are quoted over the phone only when they hear a description of the actual job requirements. This is completely acceptable and typical of service providers. If a service cannot supply a price sheet, you will have the following choices as to how you can conduct your business:

- **Tell your callers that the plumber (or electrician, locksmith, etc.,) will quote them a price after he looks at the job in**

**30**

their homes, and at that point, they can make their decision about whether or not to utilize the service (you must OK this arrangement with the service provider as well), or...

- Take your caller's name, address, phone number and job type and call it in to the plumbing service to get an estimate. After receiving a general estimate, call your customer back and arrange the job;

At first, you'll discover that it can take awhile to get used to quoting prices. After you've been running your business for awhile, however, it will become second nature to you. As you gain more and more confidence, you'll relate to customers better and may actually discover that this business is quite simple! It really is! In the beginning, of course, you'll have to learn the ropes, but after awhile, you'll turn into a pro...and the amount of money you can make will be entirely up to you!

### Beginning to advertise

Before you begin to place advertisements, **make sure that your business is ready to run.** Everything must be in place so that you can begin to receive your special five minute phone calls. You should already have a list of service providers (in this example, plumbers) who you've made arrangements with. When all of the necessary arrangements are taken care of, you can

**31**

begin running your ads. You have three basic choices:

- **Classified advertising**
- **Display advertising**
- **Direct mail**

The option that you choose will depend on a variety of factors, including where you live and how much money you can afford to advertise with. If you live in a small community that has local newspapers or larger regional papers, you can run classified ads like this one.

> **NEED A PLUMBER?** Low prices, quick service. All problems solved. Call for special free estimate. Star Plumbing (212) 555-4324

If you can afford to run a display ad, you should. Display ads give confidence to potential customers who see your ad and believe it to represent a professional, well-established operation. Of course, your advertisement can take on whatever shape or form you want it to. You can go to a professional typesetter and instruct him to include pictures or fancy fonts in your ad to make it look professional. Whatever your choice, you'll discover that display ads will bring in more phone calls than classified ads. Only use classified advertising if you have no other choice.

Remember, you're running a *professional business service!* Your ad must appear to represent a competent

**32**

operation. No one is going to call a sloppy ad or a classified ad that's placed in the wrong community. In New York City, for example, a small classified ad wouldn't work at all. It's too big a city and a larger display ad would be required.

In a small town, however, a tiny classified can generate business if the newspaper it's placed in is a small, local paper that everyone reads. You'll have to make this decision by looking through all of the local newspapers and periodicals in your area. One rule of advertising is:

**If you can afford to run a small display ad, DO IT and forget about the classifieds.**

The real truth about classified advertising is that most of them usually don't work, period. **Only advertise with classified ads if you have no other choice.** If you haven't had any experience in placing display ads, I can assure you that it need not be difficult. You can utilize the services of a professional typesetter. Most printers offer this service and can typeset your ad at a very reasonable rate. You just have to tell them what you want in the ad.

**When you design your ad, use common sense.** What type of ad would you respond to? Remember that the service industry requires a very high degree of professionalism in advertising. The people who need your services will typically want someone to come in as quickly as possible to fix the problem and leave. They need to be satisfied that the service person they'll be allowing in their home will be courteous and professional. **How do they assure this?** If they don't already have a plumber, they'll look for advertisements that appear professional and of the highest quality.

This may not always work, because even a lousy plumbing service can hire a great ad design service, but **whether it works or not,** it's a way that people select services **when they have no other choice but to do so.** Your ad should be something that people will remember. Examine the following examples and note their differences.

**Ad #1**

**Ad #2**

Advertising can make or break any business, and, since your own advertising will be the prime vehicle by which customers will contact you, the ad you run will either ruin you or make your business profitable. Therefore, **do this right! Don't cut corners on your advertising.** It should be the driving force behind your business. Use the services of a good typesetter or graphic artist, both of which can be found in your local yellow pages. In the above example, **ad number one** is clearly better that ad number two for the following reasons.

- **It creates an image of an established business. Notice the first line in the copy, "Get the Quick Fix!" At the end of the ad, the company's name is revealed as "Quick Fix Plumbing." Ad two, however, creates no memorable image for the reader to remember.**

- **The typesetting job draws attention, which means the ad will draw eyes to it. The headline with three question marks (Clogged Drain???) serves the same purpose. Ad two, however, has a bland headline.**

- **Ad one creates an air of professionalism by listing a few of the more common plumbing problems and a few benefits of using the Quick Fix Company... reasonable rates and fast service. Ad two, however, is flat when it says, "We do good work." Too bland and too juvenile.**

**Other ways to get the word out**

While advertising in local and regional newspapers with display ads is the best way to get word of your business out, there are also other ways to let people know about your services. I've come across many of these alternative advertising methods and have seen others use them with success.

- **Distributing business card ads;**
- **Using bulletin boards;**
- **Other creative means;**

There are locksmith services in New York City that have small ads printed on business cards. They leave these cards all over New York, advertising their locksmith services. When someone gets locked out of their house or apartment, they may be carrying one of these cards in their wallet, bringing business to the advertiser.

No book on the subject of advertising can tell you with 100% certainty how to advertise in your own community. Each scenario is different, and one way that may work well in Seattle might fall flat in Little Rock. Therefore, it's up to you to design your own advertising strategy. Think out a strategy well and follow it carefully.

There may be ways to advertise in your own community that aren't listed or discussed within the pages of this manual. If you feel that you can reach your target audience with innovative advertising methods, go to it. You're the boss, so your success or failure will ride on your shoulders. Plan your business carefully and you may be nicely rewarded.

## Receiving phone calls

How you answer your telephone will be important. **If possible,** have a second phone line installed in your home that you can use exclusively in your advertising. You can then answer the line with your company's name. If you cannot afford a second phone line and must advertise your home phone number, conduct yourself professionally and answer the phone with your company name. If you don't feel comfortable answering your personal line with a company name, you can answer by saying, "May I help you?" Obviously, having a second line will take care of these types of problems.

After your advertising is in place, you'll begin to discover whether or not it's effective by the number of phone calls that come in. If you receive too small an amount of calls, change your advertising. If the calls you receive are adequate, however, you can stay with your current ads and begin taking profits from your phone calls. When someone calls on your ad, answer any questions that they may have. As you begin to become more familiar with the service you provide, you'll be able to answer more and more of your customers questions without having to get back to them.

When a customer calls, he may give you the order right away. Using our plumbing service example, he may say, "I have a clogged drain...how much will it cost to fix it?" Examine your lists of service providers and, if you have any fixed prices available, give your customer a quote. If not, tell him that the plumber will give a quote after he looks over the problem, and, at that time, the customer will have the right to accept or refuse the estimate. Don't offer this option unless you've struck such an agreement with your service providers, or at least with one who's available around the time your customer needs service.

If your customer is satisfied with your answers to any questions that he may have and decides to ask for a plumber, give him an idea when the plumber will arrive and thank him for using your company. **Immediately upon hanging up the phone,** begin calling service providers from your commission list and get a plumber who's available.

After doing this a number of times, you'll discover which plumbing companies you're most comfortable with and which ones you should call last. Once one of your service providers has a plumber, instruct them to send him to your customer's home and get as general a price quote as you can, understanding the fact that the plumber hasn't seen your customer's problem in person yet. That's all there is to it! Just follow those

**38**

instructions and you'll be providing plumbers (or whatever service you've decided upon) to people all over your region.

## After the service call

After sending a plumber to your customer's home, **make a record of the transaction in your datebook.** You can't make money unless you get paid for every referral, so precise record keeping is a must. Hopefully, the plumbing services you have agreements with will be honest about issuing your commissions, but don't blindly count on it. In fact, you may decide to **call your customer** a few hours after sending the plumber to ask whether or not he was satisfied with the work.

Not only does this appear to be good business, but while you have the customer on the phone you can ask for the final total. If your customer says, "I paid $80 for the job" you would know what your commission would be. If you had a 20% commission agreement with the plumbing company, you would receive $16. Obviously, the goal in this business is to receive as many phone calls as possible. If you refer just $1,000 in plumbing services in one day, you've made $200 for a few hours work! As your business grows and grows, you can add more phone lines and bring in people to answer your calls. This means more cash profits!

## Hours of operation

Unless you devise a way to take calls 24 hours a day, you will need to establish hours of operation. If, for example, you wish to take calls from 9:00am to 5:00pm, list those hours in your advertisement.

## Other ideas for this business

If you know any plumbers personally who aren't employed with any particular service, you can strike a commission deal with them individually. Explain to them that you have a referral service and would be happy to send them out on jobs as long as they give you a cut. Typically, you can strike terrific commission deals with freelance plumbers (or other individual service providers). Some will agree to split their fees with you equally, just for the benefit of using your organization. There are many different ways to make this business work so that you receive phone calls all day long. Think about them. You may well be on your way to becoming very wealthy!

## Following local regulations

Your state or community may have laws that regulate this type of business. It would be wise to check with your local county clerk or city hall before starting your business to see whether or not there are regulations that you must follow. In most cases, the regulations, if any, will be simple to comply with. In order for your business to run successfully, it must comply with the laws of your community.

## A final word

The *Cold Cash* system can change your life completely! What you've just read is an innovative way to make money...just for receiving simple phone calls. As with any business, you will be required to put forth honest effort to achieve your goal of financial prosperity. Remember, when you start your new business, it may feel unusual at first. As you begin to get the hang of it, however, you'll discover that it eventually becomes second nature to you. Good luck to you in this and in any other endeavor that you may undertake.

# Bonus System

# Bonus System

    This bonus system is very special. It will enable you to be your own boss. As a result, you'll be able to choose your own hours and make your own decisions. You'll be in charge of your own future, not working for someone else's. There are many millionaires in the world who became wealthy because they used the very system that is contained within the pages of this book. It generates hundreds upon hundreds of millions of dollars of wealth each year. It is, quite simply, one of the world's most powerful businesses that anyone, no matter whom they may be, can participate in.

    I discovered this business quite by accident. I was at a very low point in my life financially when a very close friend showed up at my apartment and we began a discussion about making money. "Have you ever heard about commodities?" he asked me. *I had never heard much about them.* In fact, this might be where you are right now. I had always thought that the commodities markets were for very smart, even genius-type people who somehow traded food like wheat or corn on some type of "stock market" exchange. In fact, this may sound completely like yourself.

You may have *never* even heard of trading commodities. Luckily, this isn't a problem.

By the time you are finished with this book, however, you will know more than nine out of ten people on the subject. You will know enough to begin making thousands of dollars in short periods of time. In fact, there are many people who have made *thousands upon thousands of dollars* just because they made a simple five-minute phone call to their commodities broker when they realized the market was ripe for profit. I will teach you how to do this too. It's so much easier than you may think. Unlike the stock market, where any real profits are seen over months or even years, commodity trading can provide you with almost instant profits.

In fact, one of the most famous commodity traders in the United States of America is the first lady, Hillary Rodham Clinton. You may remember some time ago that the press reported that Mrs. Clinton turned *one thousand dollars* into *one-hundred thousand* dollars, virtually overnight. For a short period of time, some members of the press, who knew little about commodities, speculated that there might be some wrongdoing involved because of the huge profits that were made. Within a few days, however, it was reported that *nothing improper was done.* The huge profits that Mrs. Clinton made were completely legal and even very common in this business.

**44**

You will learn what the commodities market is and how you can profit from it by using some very simple formulas. Remember, even if you don't know a thing about the commodities markets right now, I will make it so understandable that you will completely grasp everything I am telling you. In fact, after teaching people about the commodities markets, I typically hear the same thing. People tell me that they never knew that the commodities markets could be so simple to understand and how simple it is to deal in them and make a profit. Many people, in fact, lament the fact that they have taken so long to get involved with commodities since, in reality, they are so interesting and enjoyable. Trading commodities is, for many people, a hobby as well as a business. That's how enjoyable trading can be for you.

## Is commodity trading really that simple?

I have heard many people say that commodity trading is highly risky. I used to believe that too until I began researching the commodities markets myself. I discovered that the markets are surprisingly easy to understand and that many people are quietly taking large profits as they carefully buy and sell. When dealing with any type of investment, you should proceed in a cautious manner, and the same rule applies to trading commodities. Commodity trading does involve a certain amount of risk, but you can limit that risk by using certain techniques that the commodities markets make available to help you in your trading. We will discuss some of these techniques later. You'll be surprised at how easy they are.

Although there are ways to limit your losses in commodity trading, you should never risk money that you cannot afford to lose. It is a fact of life that traders will have losing trades and the commodities markets are *not* the place to risk your entire savings or to use money that you need for necessities. Remember to *never, ever* risk money that you cannot afford to lose. There is no such thing as a sure thing, in any business.

Trading commodities can be simple because there are really only two decisions that you will have to make. While other businesses require dozens or even hundreds of decisions, trading commodities only involves two. You will merely have to decide when to buy and when to sell. That's all. What's more is that the commodity markets have rules and available strategies in place that can help you make these two simple decisions. There are trading techniques, some of which we will discuss later, that are designed to help you limit any losses that you may encounter. Unlike the common belief that only the "big boys" trade commodities, there are thousands of traders just like you and I who are quietly earning some very handsome profits by doing something that is entirely exciting and enjoyable. The commodities markets can be this way for you too!

**After I learn your system, should I begin trading immediately?**

It is imperative that upon completing your reading of this book, you begin trading commodities *on paper only* for awhile and see what lessons you can learn before you use real money. You may discover what I learned, that commodities trading can be both fun and *very* profitable if you take your time getting an education before beginning actual trading.

Many of the most wildly successful commodity traders, in fact, began trading on paper. Since you are still a novice, you should begin without risking any real money. You can learn the lessons that you need to grasp. You could read every commodity book you can find, but there are certain understandings that you can only acquire by simulating actual trading on paper.

After you read this book, begin to paper trade right away. Record what you buy or sell and track the price from the daily investment papers, such as the *Wall Street Journal* or *Investor's Business Daily*. You can see how much money you would have made or lost on each trade, and you will take a vast amount of knowledge from the experience. The key is to keep a daily journal of your trading activity and of the price of the commodity that you have chosen to paper trade with. The best thing about trading on paper is that you will develop a familiarity with commodities and with the terminology involved in trading them. The longer you paper trade, the more comfortable you will feel about commodities. Whatever you may decide to do, don't rush into trading! You should constantly further your education. It can lead to a gigantic change in your life.

## I don't know anything about commodities. Should I still get involved?

Yes! In fact, I prefer that you don't know a thing right now. Many successful traders initially knew absolutely nothing about commodities, but educated themselves through books similar to the one you are holding right now. It is important that you forget all of the speculation that you may have heard about commodities. You may have heard stories of people either *making a killing* (making a lot of money) or *getting killed* (losing a lot of money) in the commodities markets. Yes, there are people who both make and lose money, but you can drastically reduce your risk of loss through proper education. In fact, the commodities markets offer many trading tools that you can use to substantially limit your risk.

If you simply use your common sense and educate yourself about the basics of the commodities markets, you can change your entire life. Even if eight out of ten of your trades are disasters, you can live a fine lifestyle based on your two successful ones. You are never too young or too old to learn about trading commodities. You don't even to have any special kind of intelligence. In fact, most of the successful traders I know are people of particularly average intelligence. They are the types of people who no one ever thought of as being successful. Nonetheless, they found the commodities markets and discovered what I know to be a fact, that trading commodities is a wonderful business that people can get excited about. There may be no greater feeling than seeing the price of a commodity that you hold shoot through the roof, providing you with thousands of dollars in profits within a few hours or even minutes. If you are willing to learn, let us begin our journey into the fascinating world of commodity trading.

# What Commodity Trading Is

Commodity trading is perfect for the self-employed individual. You can run your commodities business from your home without any customers or employees. You can save the money you need to get started in a short amount of time. In fact, if you begin saving right now, you should be able to open your own commodities business very shortly. All you need is a relatively small amount of money to call a commodity broker and set up an account.

## When should I set up my commodity account, and how do I go about it?

You should set up your account as soon as you have saved enough money to do so. There are many commodity brokerage firms in existence today. Each brokerage house will require you to set up a commodity account before you are permitted to trade. This account is similar to a savings or checking account that you may have in a bank. When you've saved enough money to meet the brokerage house minimum requirement, send in a check to the brokerage house. Different brokerage houses have different minimum requirements to open up a commodity trading account. Some of the larger firms are not designed for the small, individual trader, and, as a result, they may require a larger initial investment. You should shop and call many brokerage firms. Their rules will vary, so it's a good idea to get as many information packages as possible from a variety of firms. Much of the information that you learn about trading, in fact, will come from the information packages that commodity brokerage firms will send to you free of charge. By looking through the *Wall Street Journal* and *Investor's Business Daily,* you will find many ads being run by commodity brokerage firms. Call as many of these numbers as you can immediately and ask for their introduction package. You'll be able to compare their commission rates and account minimum requirements and find the one that's best for you. In addition to the firms that you may call personally, the Lind/Waldock brokerage firm has a program called *Lind Plus* that is suitable for the beginner. Call them at (312) 455-3157 and ask them to send you information about opening a commodity account.

Since you are a beginner, it is imperative that you deal only with full commission brokers. *Do not deal with discount brokerage firms!* Many are merely order-taking companies that do little to help you place your order. If you should make a mistake, they will not bother to correct you. A full-service firm will take time with you on the phone to make sure that the orders you will eventually be placing are executed properly. In the long run, you will *lose* rather than gain if you try to save on brokerage commissions, *especially when trading commodities.* Every brokerage firm will charge you a commission fee when you buy and sell, so it is a fee that, while it will vary from firm to firm, is something that is unavoidable. You should try to find a firm with reasonable fees, not "bargain-basement" firms that charge very little for commission but give very little in services. You will need those services when you trade. A discount firm is not interested in helping beginning traders. Even the most experienced traders use full-commission brokers. They're better!

**Tell me more about the commodity markets.**

The commodities markets are similar in some ways to the stock market, where you choose a company and invest in it, hoping that the price of its shares will increase in value. One major difference, however, is the fact that the commodities markets do not have any companies for you to invest in. Instead, they have contracts on *goods.*

Imagine the following scene. You are walking along the street and you see a supermarket. Remembering that you need to buy some food, you enter the supermarket and look around. Suddenly, you take notice. This is not your typical supermarket at all! There are only a few products, and the prices of the products are not particularly stable. In fact, the prices often make some very wide moves. On some days, the products in this special supermarket are inexpensive, and on other days, the price moves way up. Soon, you come to understand this, so you only buy when you see that the prices are low.

This special supermarket that I've just spoken about is not such a fantasy at all. In fact, simple as it may seem, what I just told you is a pretty good description of the commodities market. The object, much like the stock market, is to buy low and sell high. You may also sell a commodity without owning it if you believe that the price of the commodity will go down, but this is seen by many to involve too high a risk of loss. This is called "selling short" and is very, very risky. Many traders never "sell short" because of this fact. It is best to buy first sell later. Selling short is too risky.

Unlike most stock market trades, *there is a time limit on commodities*. You may have as little as a one month time limit or as much as eighteen months to hold onto a commodity that you have purchased. This may sound like bad news to you, but in reality, it is not. As you begin to trade commodities, you will become less and less encumbered by the time limit. The time limit is not a secret either. When you call your commodities broker, he* will tell you when your *contract* will expire or *come due,* as it is often referred to. This is also called the *delivery month,* as each contract has an expiration date.

## What can I buy from the commodities markets?

As I mentioned earlier, one of the best pieces of advice that I could give you on the subject of the commodities markets is to begin reading a daily business newspaper. As complicated as this may seem, you will nonetheless pick up a host of information from these publications. Each of these newspapers has a commodities section where they list the daily prices of each commodity. *Investor's Business Daily* even gives daily price graphs for each major commodity. From wheat contracts and pork belly (which is used to make bacon) contracts to gold, silver and platinum contracts, you will see them all. Here is where you can become successful. Based on the many contracts available, you'll be a success in trading commodities if, by doing your research, you can locate *one* that you can say with a degree of certainty will go *up in price.* That's all there is to it! If, for example, you believe that the price of sugar will go up, you can buy a sugar contract. If you're right and the price goes up, you

---

* We use the term "he" here for the sake of brevity, but not all commodity brokers are men. Some of the most able, in fact, are women.

make money by selling the contract at a higher price.

Not all commodities are foods, either. There are contracts on precious metals and even stock market indicators. Many beginners purposely avoid investing in the metals or in the financial markets because they want to keep things simple by trading the durable commodities such as corn, sugar, wheat and soybeans. Let's say, for example, that one day you discover, through your research and what you will learn in the chapters of this book, that *pork bellies* are ready to take off. Believing that pork bellies are ready to increase in price, you would call your broker and *buy* one contract. Depending on what happens with the price, you would have a number of options to consider. We'll discuss these options later.

## What do you mean by the term contract?

Do not be confused by the term *contract*. When you are investing in the stock market, for example, you own stock in a *company*, in units called "shares". When you invest in commodities, the term *contract* is used instead of shares. You may own as little as *one* contract or as many as you can afford. This is simply the measurement used. When you receive introduction packages from the commodity brokerage houses, you will get a list of all of the commodities that are sold, as well as what one *contract* exactly contains, and the minimum amount of money that you must have in your account to buy a commodity contract.

One pork belly contract, for example, contains 38,000 pounds of pork bellies. A wheat contract contains 5,000 bushels of wheat. All other commodities contain a certain amount of product that are all represented as one *contract*. This makes things simple and concise. If you decided to invest in pork bellies, you would call your broker and inform him that you want to buy one pork belly *contract*, not 38,000 pounds of pork bellies, of course! Contract specifications will sometimes change, so it is advised that you check with your broker as to the current status of each specification.

Buying a contract is based on "margin". Margin is simply a fancy term for *credit*. If you wish to buy a commodity contract, you will only need to invest a fraction of the total contract value to control one. How much this amount is will differ with each commodity brokerage firm. When you call commodity brokerage houses to request your introductory packages, you will find out what the minimum investment is regarding different types of contracts. We will discuss margin requirements in greater depth later.

**You mentioned earlier that I could sell a commodities contract without having to actually own it. How can this be?**

This is quite easy to figure. If you believe, for example, that the price of pork bellies is going to *decrease*, you could call your broker and tell him to *sell* one contract of pork bellies. If the price goes down as you expected, you could call your broker and instruct him to *buy* one contract, which would cancel the sale and leave you with a nice profit. This is referred to as *selling short.*

Again, you can either *buy or sell* in the commodities markets. **You do not have to own a contract before you sell it.** Remember---if you believe the price of a certain contract will go *down,* you can sell it and, if it does go down, buy it back later and make a profit. I know that this may sound confusing to you, but in reality it is not. Once you grasp the idea, it is quite simple. If you choose, you could completely ignore this and simply *buy* when you think prices on a certain commodity will rise and then simply *sell* it when the price does rise. Again, you should be advised that *selling short* is very risky and opens yourself up to greater losses. We advise you to gain experience in *buying* before you attempt to *sell short.* There is no "rule" that says you must *ever* sell short. It is something that you can completely avoid while making the same amount of profits by simply buying and selling later.

# Buying your first contract

After receiving your introductory packages from the brokerage houses, decide on a firm that you feel most comfortable opening an account with. After filling out all of the necessary forms, you'll mail them off with your first account deposit. Once your account is opened, your broker will call you and inform you that you can begin trading contracts. You will then be able to call your broker and inform him about what contract you would like to buy. Hopefully, you will have been trading *on paper* for a good period of time, so some familiarity and comfort with the commodities markets will have developed.

After trading on paper, you will become familiar with the way that commodity prices move. You will learn how to spot profit opportunities, and your commodity trading will become all the more successful. Not only will you be financially successful, but you'll gain admiration from your family and friends. Commodity traders are given a large amount of reverence and respect, mostly because the overwhelming majority of people do not understand the commodities markets themselves, therefore you will be looked upon in a different way. Trading will change your life in many extraordinary ways. Best of all, it can make you a lot of money.

## I've sent a check and opened an account with a broker. What do I do now?

After opening an account with a broker, you are ready to make your first five minute phone call to place an order. *Beware!* Do not rush out and waste your money on the first opportunity that you see. Let profitable opportunities make themselves available to you. Don't chase after them! Many beginners have lost their initial investment because they imagined an opportunity that really wasn't there, or only showed traces of being there. You must proceed in a very cautious manner. After your broker calls to inform you that your account has been opened, you can wait as long as you need before placing your first order. You may also make additional deposits into your account at any time, simply by sending your broker another check.

At first, trade only one contract at a time. It would be foolish to buy multiple contracts, say wheat, pork bellies, corn, coffee and others, all at once. The fewer contracts that you have to monitor, the better. One of the best ways to educate yourself in commodity trading is to simply watch the markets work. I have a good friend who watches the financial news constantly. Merely from watching the news about commodities, he has done extremely well in the markets. He has developed a "feel" for the markets, and as a result, he is prospering. He just sits in front of the TV for a couple of hours a day and watches the Financial News Network. The "second-sense" that he has acquired by watching the commodity news has made him a lot of money.

From time to time, your broker may attempt to give you advice on what to buy. I believe it best not to solicit your broker's specific recommendations on what to buy or when to sell. You are an independent commodity trader, and, as such, you should make your own trading decisions based upon your own research. Some brokers don't know much more about how to pick a successful commodity than you do. If they were so good at trading commodities, they would spend their days trading their own accounts, not those of other people. Your broker earns a commission every time you buy and sell. This commission could be anywhere from $15 to $150, depending on the firm. Because of this, your broker would like to get his customers to trade as frequently as possible, even though this is a bad overall trading strategy. You should always proceed in a cautious and deliberate manner, despite what your broker may try to get you to do.

**I want to buy my first contract. How do I discover a commodity that I think will go up in price?**

This is the most important element in commodity trading. If only we could magically see ahead a week or two, we would all reap great wealth from every commodity trade we made. Since this is obviously not a reasonable expectation, it is imperative that you educate yourself as much as possible so that you *can*, through a proper working knowledge, accurately analyze what will happen with certain commodities. Will the price of corn go up next week? Will sugar prices take off? The more accurate your answers to these questions, the higher your profits will be.

There will be many instances, in fact, in which you will be *told* that certain commodity prices will be rising. As remarkable as this may seem, it is completely true. The national media, especially the business news, often notes that certain commodity prices stand a good chance of rising. Based on such things as droughts, floods, and supply and demand issues, the business news will often report that there is a shortage in a commodity or that there is trouble in its production.

If you watch the business news closely, you will gain many insights into commodity training. Some of your most profitable trades will come from watching the news reports. If you do not have access to a good business newscast, you may want to consider subscribing to basic cable service, where you will find many excellent newscasts, particularly those on

CNN, CNBC and FNN. Watching the business news may be a somewhat boring activity, but it will provide you with an outstanding education that can translate into abundant profits.

## What does the term "fundamental analysis" mean?

There are two types of analyses that you can use to attempt to forecast what will happen with any given commodity. The first is *fundamental analysis*, which involves such things as looking at the actual conditions that influence production of a certain commodity, such as weather conditions in the Midwest, where wheat is grown. You can buy or sell based on a report of those conditions. If, for example, you hear early reports of drought in the Midwestern wheat-growing states, you could assume that the price of wheat will rise because there will be less supply of it.

We've all been to the grocery store and seen how the prices of such commodities as orange juice can rise because there's trouble in its production. Many commodity traders have invested in the market when there were freezes in the orange-growing sections of Florida. They invested in orange juice, knowing that the freeze in Florida would create a lack of supply, thereby not meeting the demand. As a result, the commodity of orange juice becomes much more valuable.

When you receive your introductory packages from the brokerage houses, go down the complete list of commodities that are being traded. Take note of the ones that are influenced by weather conditions, such as wheat. Begin reading the daily financial newspaper in your area very closely, keeping an eye out for reports of unusual weather conditions that may affect the prices of certain commodities. If you see a situation developing where you believe weather conditions will cause the price of a certain commodity to rise, it might be a very good idea to buy a contract on that commodity.

Many traders, for example, made tremendous fortunes during the Gulf War. As our veterans fought the advancements of Saddam Hussein into the tiny nation of Kuwait, the traders knew that the war was occurring in an important oil-producing section of the world. As a result of the war, there was widespread unrest regarding oil production. In fact, most newspapers in the country carried this fact on their front pages. *This was clearly an opportunity that presented itself to the commodity trader.* The price of oil shot up furiously, and many walked away from it with fatter bankbooks.

You may be interested in other types of commodities. Perhaps, for example, you enjoy forecasting the prices of gold, silver and platinum (the "metals"). If this is the case, you can devote your time to them, instead of the agricultural commodities. Whatever commodities you eventually decide to invest in, your profits can be equally large for each commodity.

## How can I afford to purchase a commodity contract and how much money will I need?

As there are different commodities, there are different prices and specifications per contract. Using wheat as an example, there are 5,000 bushels of wheat in one contract. If, for example, the price of wheat is $3.50 *per bushel,* one contract of wheat would be worth $17,500. If commodity traders were required to raise that kind of money merely to invest in a single contract, there would be very few traders. The commodities markets, however, have created a way in which the average investor can control commodity contracts with only a fraction of that amount. Instead of having to spend $17,500 to control a contract of wheat, you only have to put up $1,000 or less! This is called *buying on margin.*

Margin requirements enable you to have a very small amount of money in your commodity account in order to control a contract that is worth much more. The *margin requirement* differs with each commodity. It may be higher depending on market conditions and on what your commodity brokerage requires. Your broker will inform you as to the minimum requirement for funds that you are required to have in your account for the various commodities. If the rates your brokerage firm requires seem unusually high, you may want to consider looking at some other brokerage firms. Each and every commodity trader buys on margin. This is not unusual. It is merely the way trading is done. Do not allow it to intimidate you.

Since you are controlling 5,000 bushels of wheat (one contract), every penny the price of a wheat contract moves is equal to *fifty dollars*. This is because there are 5,000 bushels, and a one-cent move up or down multiplied by *5,000 bushels* equals *fifty dollars*. Therefore, if the price of wheat were to rise by twenty cents, you would have a profit of one-thousand dollars! This would be an immediate return of *one-hundred percent* on your original investment!

Best of all, this can happen within the time span of a single trading day. The opposite is true as well. Every cent the price moves downward will cost you fifty dollars. If you were to purchase one contract of wheat at the price of $3.50 per bushel and the price were to drop to $3.30, your entire margin of $1,000 would be wiped out. If the price went lower than $3.30, you would lose *more* than your margin, and your broker would call to inform you that you need to place more money in your account (if it isn't there).

Fortunately, there is a way to insure that this rarely, if ever, happens. You can limit your losses by using what is called a *stop-loss order* whenever you instruct your broker to buy a contract. Therefore, when buying your wheat contract, you would instruct your broker to buy one contract of wheat at $3.50 and *place a stop-loss at $3.40.* If the price of wheat were to drop to $3.40, your broker would immediately sell your contract for you. You would maintain a loss of five-hundred dollars and no more, thanks to the stop-loss order. If the price of your commodity rises, call your broker and instruct him to move your stop-loss order up. If your $3.50 wheat contract moves to $3.80, for example, the stop-loss should be reset to $3.70. Always move your stop-loss close enough to the daily trading price so that you will not sustain wide losses.

The commodities markets also have trading rules to help you. One such rule is called the *limit move.* This simply means that the commodities markets only allow prices to move a certain amount in price before trading is stopped for the day. If, for example, you purchased a wheat contract at $3.50, the worst loss you could sustain in one trading day would be limited to whatever the market rules allow. In most wheat markets if you purchased a wheat contract at $3.50 per bushel, trading would be stopped immediately if the price managed to tumble to $3.30. This is called a *limit down* move.

A limit move applies equally to situations when the price of a contract rises too quickly. If your $3.50 contract shot up to $3.70 within a single day, trading would probably be halted. This is called a *limit up* move. One wheat contract contains 5,000 bushels of wheat, so, as was just discussed, each penny move either upward or downward equals fifty dollars. The value of a one-cent move will differ with each commodity. Your broker will provide you with a listing of the specifications of each commodity so that you know how much money a one-cent move represents.

Every trader has losing trades, but successful ones will put you on the positive side if you *limit your losses on your losing trades with the stop-loss order.* All traders experience losing trades, but the successful ones still earn large overall profits due to this important money management technique. Your goal should not be to never have a losing trade. It should be to make *overall* profits.

The importance of placing a stop-loss order with every contract that you buy cannot be overemphasized. *You will not be a successful trader* if you do not use this technique every time you place an order with your broker. When you buy a commodity contract, it is disturbing to experience a loss, but it is even more disturbing to lose everything because you did not use the tools available to assist you with your trading.

**I notice that the commodity price listings in the newspaper have many**

**67**

different months listed for each commodity. If I want to buy a commodity contract, do I have to tell my broker what month I want the contract to be in?

The prices of wheat that are listed in the daily investment newspapers will look something like the following price chart. As you can see, the price of wheat is listed several times on a monthly basis.

PRICE CHART FOR CHICAGO GRAIN
Wheat - 5,000 bushels; $ per bu

| MONTH | OPEN | HIGH | LOW | CLOSE | OP. INT. |
|---|---|---|---|---|---|
| July | 3.49 | 3.49 | 3.47 | 3.48 | 4,372 |
| Sep | 3.60 | 3.61 | 3.58 | 3.59 | 5,617 |
| Dec | 3.74 | 3.75 | 3.71 | 3.73 | 4,328 |
| Mar | 3.89 | 3.90 | 3.86 | 3.87 | 2,922 |
| May | 4.10 | 4.12 | 4.09 | 4.10 | 1,073 |
| July | 4.22 | 4.23 | 4.22 | 4.22 | 512 |

There is very good reason for this. Commodities are actual things. As a trader, of course, you will never see the actual commodity. You are merely attempting to profit from it by owning control of it (a contract) before the actual delivery date. If you were to hold on to your wheat contract until the last day of the contract month you would have to assume delivery, which is not at all what you want to do.

You should watch all of your commodity positions closely so that you assure yourself of selling your contracts before the last day of the delivery month. If, for example, you owned one **July** wheat contract, you would probably have to liquidate your position before the last day in July. A competent broker will call you to advise you that your delivery date is approaching so that you can liquidate your position before that time. If you do not want to sell your commodity contract but the expiration date is approaching, you can tell your broker to sell your contract and buy one in a month that is further away. This is called a "roll-over" as you are taking a contract that has gotten old and sold it in order to purchase a new one, therefore giving yourself more time to hold onto the commodity.

Since commodities are actual things, they need to be stored somewhere. As you can see in the price chart, the prices for wheat are higher as each delivery month is further away. The price is higher because storage charges for the actual commodity are added on to the price. When purchasing a contract, you must tell your broker what contract month you wish to be in. Choosing the best month to trade in is typically an easy decision, although you should consider it carefully. You do not want to purchase a contract that has a **near** delivery month. If you did, you would have to liquidate your position within a few short weeks. This would leave you with a restricted profit opportunity. You want to sell your contract *before* the expiration date (delivery date), and you should leave enough time before delivery is due so that you can make a profit.

Your decision on what month to buy should also consider the total number of contracts that are *open*. Looking back to our price chart, the last column is listed as "Op. Int." This stands for *open interest* and refers to the number of commodity contracts that are being traded. As you can see, the most activity occurs in the second month listed, September. There are 5,617 open contracts. The nearest month, July, has slightly **less** because it is the delivery month, and traders are beginning to liquidate (sell) their positions.

As the contract months get further away, there is less open interest. Since there is less activity in the far months, you would have less traders to sell to if you traded in those months, and there would be less activity. Traders often buy commodity contracts in distant months when they believe that the price will not rise for awhile, so they want to have contracts that won't expire for some time. Additionally, you should rarely, if ever, purchase a contract in the month of delivery. You would have to sell almost immediately upon buying the contract to avoid the delivery date. It is probably best to buy a contract in the second or third month from delivery, because there is more activity occurring. On the price chart, the delivery month is always the first month listed, as it is closest to the date that you are actually reading the newspaper listing.

For illustration purposes, I have placed a box around the second and third months from delivery as they appear on the price chart above. Notice how high the open interest is, as the second and third months from delivery are typically very busy. These would be the ideal months in which to trade if you wanted to buy a wheat contract, or any commodity for that matter. Of course, if the second and third months from delivery do *not* have a high open interest, you should avoid them, but they are typically the most active, and therefore the best, months in which to trade commodities.

The price chart lists the price of wheat contracts *per bushel*. The trading day's *opening price, high and low prices for the day, close for the day, and the number of open contracts for the contract month* are all listed in different columns. Once you own a commodity contract, you will find yourself looking through your newspaper's commodity price charts to plot your progress. You will discover that learning to read the commodity listings is quite simple and uncomplicated.

When deciding what contract month to trade in, simply remember not to trade in a month that is too close to delivery *and* to trade in a month with a good number of available contracts (open interest). You don't need to become overly worried about the delivery date. Just be aware of what it is. If you find yourself holding a contract with a very near delivery date, you can ask your broker to do a **roll-over**. Simply call your broker and tell him you want to sell your contract and buy one in a further contract month. Traders do this all the time, and it is an easy way to push the delivery date further away.

**If I should see a profit opportunity developing, such as the ones you mention, what should I do next?**

No one knows what the future may bring. As a new commodity trader, you may find yourself faced with many different kinds of opportunities, perhaps similar in many ways to the ones I've mentioned here. Assume, for example, that you are watching the evening news and the news anchor reports that there is widespread unrest in the Middle East and that fear is spreading regarding the supply of oil. Now that you are a trader, you'll be watching the news from a new angle...a profit angle.

Seeing that there is widespread unrest in oil, you know that there is a considerable chance that the price of crude oil will shoot up imminently. Crude oil is traded on the Chicago Board of Trade, which opens at 8:30am Central Time. (The commodities markets have many different exchanges and trading hours, just as the stock market has the New York Stock Exchange and others. For practical purposes, this means little since your broker has access to all of the various commodity exchanges).

You've been doing your research and you know that this appears to be a superb opportunity to jump into the market. It is time to call your broker and buy a contract. You could, of course, begin by purchasing more than one contract, but it is best to only buy one at first. If you buy a single contract and the price goes against you, your amount of loss will be less. If, however, you buy multiple contracts and things turn down, you'll lose a lot more. Unlike the stock market, where investors purchase hundreds or even thousands of shares of stock, it is not advantageous to buy multiple commodity contracts at the beginning of a trade. The old adage *better safe than sorry* surely applies to commodity traders.

Once you are connected to your broker, you will need to inform him that you would like to buy a commodity contract. By now, you should have checked to make sure that you have sufficient funds in your account to cover your margin requirement. We'll use *crude oil* for the sake of our illustration. When you call to instruct your broker to buy a contract, you will need to tell him what your account number is, what commodity you are buying, what month you want and where you would like your stop-loss order placed. Therefore, your order might sound something like this:

**"BUY ONE JULY CRUDE OIL CONTRACT at $19.30 AND PLACE A STOP-LOSS at $18.80"**

Your broker can buy the contract "at the market" (which is whatever the current selling price is on the trading floor) or, you can request a certain price. In this case, your broker will only buy a contract of July Crude Oil for you if the market touches your asking price of $19.30. If you want to buy a contract at the best price, simply tell your broker the following:

**"BUY ONE JULY CRUDE OIL CONTRACT at the market AND PLACE A STOP-LOSS fifty-cents BELOW THE PURCHASE PRICE"\***

As was mentioned previously, the amount of a one-cent move will vary with each commodity. With crude oil, one contract contains 1,000 barrels. Therefore, a one-cent move per barrel would equal ten dollars in this case. It is important that you be aware of the differences in each commodity. You should not be confused by this way of buying a contract. These are simply uniform terms that are used by commodity traders to make your trades easier, quicker and more exact. They are all very simple to understand and grasp. Imagine, in fact, how confusing placing an order would be if there were no specific terms to use. When you receive introduction packages from commodity brokerage firms, they will easily explain

---

\*    This is the exact way to tell your broker what to order.  If, however, you aren't sure of exactly what to say, you can easily ask your broker to help you place your order.

exactly how to place an order. As you use them in your paper trading, you will become extremely comfortable with them. By using a full commission broker, you will be given assistance to make sure that your order is executed exactly as you would like it to be.

Upon placing your order, your broker will repeat it back to you. Listen closely to make sure that there are no errors. If you are not sure that your trade is being executed properly, insist that it be repeated back to you. You should only hang up the telephone when you are absolutely sure that your order has been entered properly. Within minutes of calling your broker, he will return your call and let you know that your trade has been completed.

Once your trade is completed, you can call your broker to ask what the price is. You do not want to bother your broker, so you may decide to subscribe to a quotation service that gives you prices throughout the day. Or, you can watch the financial news during commodity trading hours to watch your specific commodity price. The daily investment papers will also include a listing of the prices of each commodity, similar to the listing in this chapter.

# The Power of Technical Analysis

If the only tool you could use to forecast price movements was fundamental analysis, you would be waiting around a long time. Opportunities *do* present themselves but sometimes they're slow in revealing themselves. Floods, droughts and orange freezes only happen so often, so you will need to use other tools to locate profit opportunities.

Thankfully, there is an answer to this dilemma. *Technical analysis* is the most powerful trading tool you have at your disposal. Many commodity traders initially saw only modest profits from their trading until they got an education in technical analysis. Most of the famous commodity fortunes were made directly as a result of using this mighty weapon.

Best of all, technical analysis can be quite simple! The big shots involved in trading commodities do not want you to know this. They enjoy having people believe that technical analysis is too complicated for the average person to understand. In fact, technical analysis is one of the easiest way for you to profit in trading commodities.

The *Wall Street Journal* and *Investor's Business Daily* publish daily charts and graphs that illustrate the movement of a commodity price. Based on these charts, certain patterns in price movement can alert you to the fact that a certain commodity is ready to take off, presenting a terrific investment opportunity. What is so special about the charts is that they will enable you to recognize opportunities that you would have been unable to locate through fundamental analysis, so it is imperative that you further your education by researching this method in greater depth.

We will examine one of the most basic of these movements here, but you should invest in a good technical analysis course that will educate you as to the dozens of patterns on a price graph that can reveal that it is time to buy or sell a contract. This cannot be overemphasized. Learning about technical analysis will be one of the best investments that you could ever make. The small investment you make in a complete commodity course can be returned one-hundred fold to you, all in gigantic profits. I do know that the largest profits that I have seen in commodity trading has come from traders who have used this powerful, yet simple, commodity forecasting technique.

In a world where people tend to spend money very frivolously, getting an education on this subject would be a very wise investment. It would be foolish of me to suggest that I can adequately cover the entire subject in the space that we have here, because a good technical analysis education takes serious study. I would be remiss if I led you to believe otherwise. Having said that, allow me to give you an example of how powerful and simple technical analysis can be.

The chart at the end of this chapter maps the progress of wheat. Notice how wheat is going forward with very little up or down movement. It rises a little and then falls and then rises again. This is called a *tunnel.* I have drawn a straight line on the top and on the bottom of the tunnel so that you can see it better. It is called a *tunnel* because it looks like a tunnel! See how simple it is? It's simple, but it's as powerful as any army that has ever walked this earth.

You can make **a lot of money** in commodity trading by using it. Here's how: When you see a tunnel developing on a commodity chart, draw lines around it like I have. *As soon as the price of the commodity moves above the tunnel, the commodity could be ready to rise substantially.* Keep watching your commodity charts, which can be found daily in *Investor's Business Daily.* When the price goes through the top of the tunnel, you have a chance of making a handsome profit if you *buy* immediately.

I have just given you one example of technical analysis. There are many, many additional technical analysis tools, just as simple and insightful, that you can use to make large profits in the commodities markets. In fact, there are dozens of them, each virtually as simple as the one that I have illustrated here. Don't be fooled by their simplicity. They are the most powerful tools that you have available to you in trading commodities. Your largest profits will be made when you make a buying decision based on technical analysis. It is a tool that you must use if you want to become a very successful trader.

In addition to the chart that is at the end of this chapter, there are many other configurations that exist that are as powerful and simple as the "tunnel" technique. They go by many names, and they are all designed to forecast what will happen to a commodity price. Since the whole idea of trading commodities is to forecast when a price will rise (so that you can buy it before it does), technical analysis is a very important tool.

Your broker can even provide you with charts that you can graph on your own. Technical analysis is a very straightforward way to forecast commodity prices. Plus, when you already own a commodity contract, technical analysis can help you decide when to sell it before the bottom falls out of the price and you lose all of your profits. It is an education that is worth pursuing!

# Exhibit A

## September Wheat $ per bushel

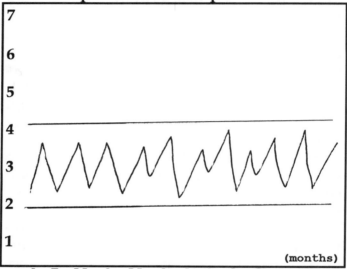

Notice how the price goes up and down within the three dollar range, creating a tunnel. When the price rises above the tunnel, it's time to buy. It's a simple, but powerful way to predict your trades! If you already own a commodity contract, you can determine when to sell by watching when the price moves below the tunnel, thereby forecasting a downward trend.

# A Final Word

Trading commodities is perhaps one of the most exciting business endeavors that you can aspire to. Commodity traders are looked upon with great respect, and people constantly admire their knowledge and experience, both as traders and as simple human beings. You cannot help but to become a more sophisticated individual when you study the commodity markets. You elevate your knowledge and sharpen your analytical skills, usually without even knowing you're doing it!

Commodity Trading is a real business. It can make you some very real money, and, if you should decide to continue your education, there will be many rewards in store for you. You don't need to become confused or intimidated by your education. There are, unfortunately, some commodity traders (not the majority) who enjoy the fact that people think of them as being especially intelligent merely because they understand the commodity markets.

This book has proven that a commodity education need not be confusing or difficult. Don't let some people tell you that you can't understand commodities. You can understand them.

As an author, I can tell you that I personally never thought that I could understand commodities. Because of this belief, for years I never tried to learn. Then, someone helped **me** learn, and now, I help others understand and make money in trading commodities.

An author's greatest accomplishment is if he or she can reach others with their words. I hope and pray that I have reached you. I hope that I have sparked an interest deep in your soul. If you now have an interest in the commodity markets, let me urge you not to let it pass by! The desire you feel to learn more is a power that can propel you towards great and exciting riches.

I personally know many people who have made substantial moneys by trading commodities. Some of these people trade commodities full time. They make a living at it. Other people enjoy trading commodities on the side. Whatever manner in which you decide to trade, I am sure you'll agree that trading commodities is one of the most, if not **the most exciting business in the world!**

It always amazes me how different commodity traders are from each other. Most people think of a commodity trader as a man in a conservative business suit, walking down the street with a briefcase. It isn't so! I've met commodity traders who were men, women, young, old, black, white, tall, short, and people who've never worn a business suit in their entire lives.

It's people like you...the ordinary, hardworking man or woman, who is the real backbone in this business.

As one who has seen the great profits made by ordinary people in trading commodities, I urge you to continue your education. I know so many capable people who have a lot of fear in their lives. They tell me, "I am only an ordinary person. I can't make any real money trading commodities." I always tell them the same thing. You're only limited by what you THINK you're limited to.

Don't sell yourself short! If the idea of trading commodities sounds good to you, I assure you that great rewards can be in your future. Your life can change overnight. All it takes is one good trade, and it happens everyday, to all types of people, and I would like it to happen to you. Allow me to ask you a question. "Would you like to become a trader?"

If your answer is "yes," I would like to congratulate you on your new job title. You are a "trader" now! Your level of success will depend on how complete your commodity education is. The good news is that YOU are in the driver's seat now. The decisions are all yours. You are on your way to becoming your own boss. You are on your way to no longer having to take orders from a boss.

You are also on your way to achieving your dream. Whatever your dream is, you can attain it. If you have a dream to open up a new restaurant, you can get the money to do this by trading commodities! If you have a dream to buy a brand new car, the car of your dreams, you can achieve it by trading commodities. **Whatever your dream, you can achieve it by trading commodities.**

## "This is amazing! There's no other word to describe the power of this very real money making system."

Just the other day, I was in the hospital visiting a loved one. What I saw completely shocked me. I'd like to tell you a little bit about it. As I walked into the hospital, I saw many different rooms. The person I was visiting was in one room, but in all the other rooms, there were numerous elderly people lying sickly in their beds.

The sight alone was very depressing. I think you know what I mean. There was a man there who kept groaning, "Nurse! Please...the pain is so terrible!" The man was quieted after the nurse came, but seeing these people in pain and unhappiness had a profound effect on me.

"Will this happen to me?" I asked. I just couldn't shake the images from my mind. I thought about those elderly men and women and wondered about the dreams they must have had as human beings. I'm sure they always wanted the things most of us hope for. A family. Friends. Happiness. And, enough money to live (and die) with dignity.

As most people do, I'm sure these people had tried to succeed in their own lives. I just know they tried different things to get ahead and to be financially independent. And yet, they lie in a hospital bed with only sadness and no more time to make things right. Imagine what they would give for just one more try at life...how differently they would do things!

My visit to the hospital changed me in a way. To be quite frank with you, **it made my desire for money get even stronger.** I want to be able to buy the best care, the best home and,

**85**

yes, the very best life! A life that I could guiltlessly enjoy in comfort and in peace.

A 9 to 5 job is basically like giving your life away to someone else. I remember when I worked 9 to 5. I would get up in the morning and groan (literally). I knew that having to use all of my energy and money just to work for my boss and make him rich was a sure-fire way to unhappiness and sadness. I knew that if I kept working 9 to 5, I would eventually find myself an old man who never took time out to make his own dreams come true. I didn't want this to happen at any cost.

I started buying more different business plans and I even tried to succeed a few times. But every week, I was still up at 7 o'clock in the morning, having to get to my boss's office before he would get angry at me for being late. And then, all day, as thoughts of my own future swam in my mind, he would bark orders at me. And every order I carried out, I knew it was cash in **his** pocket, not mine!

After searching and searching for about three years (and getting more depressed and disgusted with every new day), I came across a new system that changed my life. A friend asked me, "Have you ever heard about trading commodities?" To be honest about it, I never had. Then, my friend explained it to me.

Commodity trading isn't like investing in the stock market. Many people would have you believe that only the big shot traders make money in the commodities markets. This is not so! If only the big Wall Street type traders made money in the commodities markets, it would go completely out of business. It's the *little guy* that makes the real backbone of this business. There are thousands of individuals just like **you** who are quietly doing their homework and putting away some very handsome profits. You never see their names in the paper, but as sure as the sky is blue, they are there...thousands of little investors who supply themselves and their families with a very, very comfortable living.

In trading commodities, you buy contracts of goods. You never see these goods. You simply make money buying and selling over the phone. You can trade corn, cattle, wheat, oil, silver or whatever! I'll explain all of this to you in the most easy-to-understand language available today. As an educator, I understand the importance of saying things in such a way so that my students understand them. I know you want to make big bucks trading commodities (even if you don't understand them right now).

I'm not going to send you something you don't understand. Believe me when I tell you, I've been where you are. I know the circumstances you're in, because I've been there. Now, I hang out with men and women who've literally made thousands of dollars within one day! Best of all, these people are no smarter than you or I, and they started out with a relatively small investment. They took that investment and, using the easy techniques found in the course, completely changed the entire course of their lives. They live in comfort and luxury because they decided to get serious and learn the easy techniques that show you how to succeed in trading commodities. Those techniques are in the course I'm offering to you right now.

Before you can personally earn these profits, however, a complete commodity trading education is essential. You must know *everything* about the commodity markets. Again, this information is simple and easy, and, by learning it, you'll be able to rack up some very handsome

**87**

checks (profit!) for you and your family. You'll be able to live the life you've always dreamed of...buying the nicest cars, homes and luxuries. Past performance isn't an indicator of future results, but I'll show you how to **maximize your profits** for an all-out amazing new freedom in life. That means you can say good-bye to your annoying boss. It also means you can impress the hell out of your family and friends with your new career as a commodity trader!

Most people are just too silly and scared to think they could ever be successful with commodity trading. They don't have the "backbone" to take a chance. They'd rather "play it safe" and sit back and hope they hit the lottery some day soon. But it never happens and they wind up with little time left in life, wondering why they never made it big.

For example, many self-made commodity millionaires became wealthy because they used the powerful technique of technical analysis. Technical analysis is revered as commodity trading's most powerful tool. Merely by looking at a simple-to-read price graph, even a beginning trader can pinpoint when a certain commodity is ready to take off and produce big money profits.

You can do this too. In fact, I've never met an individual who couldn't understand technical analysis. It can be as simple as analyzing whether or not a line is going up or down on a price graph. In fact, many traders adore technical analysis and make it a personal hobby because it can be so fascinating. One of the major advantages of using technical analysis is that it can take the "guess work" out of estimating when a commodity's price will rise. Instead of having to wonder whether or not a profit opportunity is really there, you can see it right on the price graph. You simply need to know what the formations look like.

The course doesn't stop there. It's a **complete** education in commodity trading, and it'll show you every which way to begin trading with a powerful knowledge that can blow your income sky high. Let me give you a quick example. If you shop in a supermarket, you know how the price of coffee, sugar and orange juice can change very quickly. Sometimes, orange juice is cheap, sometimes it sells for outrageously high prices. After awhile, you get a "feel" for the price.

You know when it's going to go up, or at least you make a pretty good guess. Well, orange juice is a commodity that's traded on the markets! Buy it when it's **low** and sell it when it's high and **you've made good money...real good!** Best of all, orange juice is something that people always need and will always buy and drink, so you know it isn't going to go broke, like some companies on the stock market.

### You Can Make a lot of Money Trading Commodities by Getting a Full Education

For a complete education on commodity trading, allow me to introduce our newest course, *The Complete Guide to Trading Commodities: How to Profit Using Advanced Forecasting and Strategy Techniques.* The course contains nearly 150 full-sized pages of instruction plus a total of three hours of frank discussion on two cassette tapes. This is literally a "first class" course all the way. But enough about the beauty of the course. It's *what you can earn* by taking the course that will change your life.

You'll learn everything you need to know about the commodity markets to begin trading immediately. I'll show you how to get a good broker, how to open an account, and what to say in your five-minute phone calls when you buy and sell your commodities. My course is unlike any other commodity trading course on the market today. Just take a walk to your local book store and ask for a book on commodity trading. I assure you, what you'll see will confuse and intimidate you. It will even bore you! It's like the author of the book was writing it for people who already knew everything about trading commodities. No book on the market takes you by the hand and teaches you in a simple and understandable manner. My course, however, is specifically written in a particularly simple style. You will learn...

- Exactly what the commodity markets are;

- The one thing you should always look for on a commodity chart that can make you an overnight millionaire;

- What a *breakout* is on a commodity chart and how it can bring you *enormous* profits;

- What *pyramiding your commodities profits* is and how it can make you a complete fortune;

- What an *option* is and how a tiny investment can make you large profits with limited risk (perfect if you only have a small amount of money to invest);

- What to look for on a commodities chart that will tell you to *sell or else;*

- What days you should *absolutely stay away* from the commodities market;

- What the one thing your broker will always try to get you to do *but you never should;*

**90**

- PLUS numerous easy-to-read charts, graphs and illustrations that will make technical analysis easily understandable and workable;

- HOW TO TRADE commodities if you don't have a lot of money to spend...and still make nice profits;

- THE STUPIDEST mistake the beginners make in trading commodities...and why you must avoid it at all costs;

- PLUS much, much more! (Remember---this is the COMPLETE Guide to Trading Commodities!).

Many famous commodity traders hold seminars that cost *hundreds of dollars a plate* just to give you the information provided in the course. Plus, the way that they present their information is very difficult to understand. That's why we've included two double-length cassette tapes with the course. By following the discussion, you'll enhance your understanding of commodity trading like never before. What you will hear will make commodity trading so understandable that you can begin using these new forecasting techniques immediately upon completion of the course.

I've asked a few people I consider to be "idiots" to read this course, and even they sound like millionaire traders when they're done! Believe me, your newfound knowledge will impress your family and friends and will provide you with the most successful, yet simple, weapons ever developed in trading commodities for a profit. Many big shot traders don't want you to have this course. They love making people think that they're "geniuses" and "intellectuals" because of what they do. I'm blowing away their fake costumes by showing everybody how easy it is. I'm happy to report that because of this course alone, many people now know the truth about trading and how easy it is to understand everything you need to know.

This course is a complete education in commodity trading. After finishing it, I won't contact you again with new commodity book offers. Everything you need to know about commodity trading will be included in the course, so there's nothing more to buy. Every question that you may now have will be answered in a simple and completely understandable manner. After completing the course, you will know as much about trading commodities as any commodity millionaire (but remember---they don't want you to know that!).

At the conclusion of the course, you will have the option of completing an examination on what you've learned. The examination is included with the course. My assistants will grade it for you and, if you pass successfully, you will be awarded a diploma certifying that you have completed the City Commodity School course in trading commodities for money. The diploma is presented on striking parchment and is suitable for framing. But more importantly, when returning your completed exam, our educators will show you where you should review the course to gain **maximum money profits!**

## If you don't like the course, I'll send someone to pick it up and I'll rush you a refund by return mail!

*The Complete Guide to Trading Commodities* comes with an unconditional thirty-day money back guarantee. **Buy the course, study it and put it to use.** I'm so sure that you'll be thrilled with what you've learned that I'm going to make an unheard of guarantee! The day you receive the course, look it over. If you don't agree that everything I've said here is completely **true and honest,** give me a call at my offices and I'll send someone to pick it up and I'll rush you a refund by return mail (less s/h costs)! You can call me anytime *for any reason whatsoever* within the 30-day period and I'll refund your purchase price ! That's how sure we are that the course will put **real money** in your pocket by trading commodities. You either make big money trading commodities or I send someone to pick it up! You can't lose!

The complete course, including the huge complete commodity trading manual, Three-hours of discussion on two cassette tapes and the final examination can be yours for only $129.95. I believe this is the lowest price of **any** commodities trading course on the market today. To order, print your name and address on a piece of paper with the words "Trading Commodities for Money" and send $129.95 (plus $10 heavy-weight first class shipping and handling, total $139.95) to:

## City Books Publishing Company
18 Greenwich Avenue, New York, NY 10011

# Visa/Mastercard/Amex
## Call TOLL FREE 24 hours a Day
## 1(800) 611-6101 dept. TCC-88
Customer Service (212) 243-1793
Monday to Friday, 10:30am to 6:30pm, EST